Foundations – Faith Life Essentials
Final Judgment

© 2010 Derek Prince Ministries–International
This edition DPM-UK 2020
ISBN 978-1-78263-560-4
Product Code B109D

Derek Prince Ministries
www.derekprince.com

EXPANDED
VERSION:
GROUP
STUDY

Final
Judgement

DPM

DEREK PRINCE MINISTRIES - UK

Contents

About This Study Series

The Bible is God's Word and our "instruction manual" to find the path to salvation in Jesus. It then shows us how to walk with Him once we have come to know Him. Logically, therefore, it is a hugely important part of our challenge as Christian believers to study the Word of God.

A sad fact is that very often we forget most of what we have heard quite quickly! As a result, what we have heard often has little impact on the way that we continue to live.

That is why we developed these Study Guides. As Derek Prince has said numerous times in his teaching, "It is a general principle of educational psychology that children remember approximately 40 percent of what they hear; 60 percent of what they hear and see and 80 percent of what they hear, see and do."

This Study Guide is intended to help you to assimilate the truths that you have heard into both your head and into your heart so that they become more than just knowledge and will begin to change the way that you live.

Living the Christian life

This study is part of a series of 10 messages, based on the doctrinal foundation of the Christian Life described in Hebrews 6:1-2 which says,

Therefore, leaving the discussion of the elementary principles of Christ, let us go on to perfection, not laying again the foundation of repentance from dead works and of faith

toward God, of the doctrine of baptisms, of laying on of hands, of resurrection of the dead, and of eternal judgment.

This mentions six specific foundation stones that we need to lay before we can build a dwelling place for the Lord in our hearts and lives:

1. Repentance from dead works
2. Faith towards God
3. The doctrine of baptisms – John's baptism, Christian baptism and baptism in the Holy Spirit
4. Laying on of hands
5. Resurrection of the dead
6. Eternal judgment

When this teaching is applied in your life, with faith, we believe that it will deepen your relationship with God and enable you to live a truly successful Christian life.

How to Study

Each book contains a QR-code (or DVD) that links you to a talk by Derek Prince, the transcript of the talk and questions for personal application or to be discussed in a group setting.

Each video is about an hour long, divided in three parts. Set aside a reasonable length of time to read the Introduction, then watch or read Derek's teaching, and finally come back to the Study Guide to reflect on the Study Questions or to discuss them with your study group.

Once you have completed this series you will find that you have an excellent summary of the teaching. This will help you to share the content with others, whether to a friend, home group or congregation. The more you share the truths you are learning, the more they will become part of your own life and testimony.

Group Study

This study guide has been developed for use by small groups as well as by individuals.

Simply proceed through the material as a team, reflect on the questions and explore the statements together for a rich and rewarding experience.

Scripture to Memorize

In this book, we have chosen key Scriptures for memorization. They will relate in some way to your overall study. Memorizing them will place a spiritual sword in your hands which you, by the Holy Spirit, will be able to use in times of spiritual conflict.

The Word of God has supernatural power for those who will take the time and effort to "hide it in their hearts" by memorizing and meditating on it. As God's Word is hidden in your heart, it becomes constantly available to you for reference, comfort, correction and meditation. Put simply, it becomes part of your life.

Look up the verse in your own Bible and write it in the space provided. You will want to write and say this verse out loud several times until you are confident you know it well. Take time to meditate on the words and their application to your life. As a group, you could talk briefly about the meaning of the verse and its relevance to the lesson or share how you applied it.

You will be asked to recall your Memory Work at the end of the book.

Eternal Judgment – an Introduction

Imagine playing a game where you didn't know all the rules or taking part in a sports competition where you didn't know the criteria against which you were to be judged. When you came to see your score at the end you would be so disappointed because, you'll think to yourself, "If only I had known how I was going to be scored I could have done things differently."

That is the very reason why God has told us in the Bible how we will be judged so that we can live our lives accordingly here on earth. In this study, you will be examining what the Scriptures have to say about the final judgments: how many there are; who will stand in judgment at which point; what the basis of judgment is and much more.

These judgments will take place regardless of any other factors because God has determined it in His Word. People may react differently to learning about the final judgment, but ultimately, if you humble yourself before God and the Bible, foreknowledge of this vitally important subject enables you to live the right life now rather than facing regret later.

Remember that judgment can be a very good thing for those who have received Jesus' death, burial and resurrection as their own and followed God's ways during their time on earth. If you do what God requires, judgment will be a glorious day for you, but for those who don't fit that category it will be a great and terrible day.

This is the last message in the Foundation – Faith Life Essentials series.

Watch the Derek Prince video teaching *Final Judgment* on YouTube. Scan the QR-code or visit dpmuk.org/foundations.

This video has been divided into three sections, following the chapters in this book. You will find the links to these sections when you tap the 'down arrow' to expand the information about the video.

SCRIPTURES TO MEMORIZE

Write down these verses and try to memorize them.

2 Corinthians 5:10

---

1 Peter 1:17

We are going to answer
to God personally only for
what we did in life.

Final Judgment

Final (or eternal) judgment is the sixth and last doctrine of the six foundational doctrines mentioned in Hebrews 6:1–2:

1. Repentance from dead works
2. Faith toward God
3. The doctrine of baptisms
4. Laying on of hands
5. Resurrection of the dead
6. Eternal judgment.

This book is the final study in these doctrines. In our study previous to this one, Resurrection of the Body, we began to move out of the realm of time and on into eternity. Eternity does not merely consist of a very long period of time. It is a totally different realm of being, scarcely within the grasp of our human understanding.

There are two main ways in which God brings judgment on people. The first is His judgments in history; the second is His eternal judgments, which is the subject of this book. Eternal judgments are those judgments which confront us as we step out of time into eternity.

Distinguishing between the two types of judgments is necessary; otherwise we might be confused by what seem to be conflicting statements in the Scripture. To clarify the differences, we will begin by considering God's judgments in history.

Judgments in History

The first judgment of God in history involves bringing blessing or punishment on succeeding generations according to the way the former generation has responded to God. In Exodus 20 we have a very clear example of God's historical judgments. In this portion of the Ten Commandments God says:

> "You shall not make for yourself a carved image—any likeness of anything that is in heaven above, or that is in the earth beneath, or that is in the water under the earth; you shall not bow down to them nor serve [worship] them. For I, the Lord your God, am a jealous God, visiting the iniquity of the fathers upon the children to the third and fourth generations of those who hate Me, but showing mercy to thousands, to those who love Me and keep My commandments."
> Exodus 20:4–6

The sin of idolatry, which is the greatest of all sins, carries with it a judgment that extends to the succeeding three or four generations. These are judgments in history for which there are countless examples in the history of Israel and of other nations that have been involved in idolatry.

Jeremiah also deals with this question of God's judgment in history. In a prayer that he prayed to the Lord, Jeremiah said:

> "You show lovingkindness to thousands, and repay the iniquity of the fathers into the bosom of their children after them—the Great, the Mighty God, whose name is the Lord of hosts."
> Jeremiah 32:18

Jeremiah says that God repays the iniquity of the fathers into the succeeding generations. This also is a judgment in history or in time. This same generational principle also applies to God's blessing on the righteous. In Psalm 103, David says:

> But the mercy of the Lord is from everlasting to everlasting on those who fear Him, and His righteousness to children's children, to such as keep His covenant, and to those who remember His commandments to do them.
> Psalm 103:17–18

There is a promise of God's blessing and righteousness to "children's children"—to succeeding generations. Stop to consider the fact that the way we conduct ourselves and relate to God not only affects us, but it may also affect successive generations. This very significant and important principle needs to be kept in mind. We can, in some way, be answerable for either the blessing or the suffering of succeeding generations.

The principle is an obvious fact of experience. For example, a child born to alcoholic parents starts, as they say, with two strikes against him. It is not the child's fault, but the judgment of God on those parents will naturally filter down through succeeding generations. It is, of course, the mercy of God that this generational judgment can be nullified when an individual comes to the Lord, because he has become part of a new family with a new Father.

Eternal Judgment

There is another kind of judgment of God that the writer of Hebrews calls "eternal judgment." This type of judgment affects our destiny in eternity. The principles of eternal judgment are completely different, and these are stated by God to Ezekiel:

*The word of the Lord came to me again, saying, "What do
you mean when you use this proverb concerning the land of
Israel, saying: 'The fathers have eaten sour grapes, and the
children's teeth are set on edge'?"*
Ezekiel 18:1–2

Ezekiel says the children are suffering for the sins of the fathers.

*"As I live," says the Lord God, "you shall no longer use this
proverb in Israel. Behold, all souls are Mine; the soul of the
father as well as the soul of the son is Mine; the soul who sins
shall die."*
verses 3–4

God is not talking about historical judgments here, but about the
judgment of every individual soul as it steps out of time into eternity.
At this point, every soul bears responsibility only for the life that it has
led and the soul that sinned shall die for its own sin. That is repeated
in verse 20, where God is still more emphatic:

*"The soul who sins shall die. The son shall not bear the guilt
of the father, nor the father bear the guilt of the son.
The righteousness of the righteous shall be upon himself,
and the wickedness of the wicked shall be upon himself."*

When we step out of time into eternity, we are no longer being
judged for the sins or blessings of our parents or forebears. We are
going to answer to God personally only for what we did in life. The
righteousness of the righteous will be upon him and the wickedness
of the wicked will be upon him.

The book of Ecclesiastes tells us: "Where the tree falls, there it shall
lie" (11:3). The condition you are in when you die will determine your
condition throughout eternity. This is eternal judgment and it is a
very solemn thought.

When my book 'Foundational Truths for Christian Living' originally came out, it was in seven separate, small volumes, the last one being Eternal Judgment, which was similar to this book. I remember with amusement that when we would display these books for people to buy, they would almost invariably pick up the first six, but somehow decline to buy number seven. They just did not like the title, Eternal Judgment.

However, whether we like it or not, we must face the reality of eternal judgment because "it is appointed for men to die once, but after this the judgment" (Hebrews 9:27).

Five Principles of God's Judgment

We will now consider the five principles of God's eternal judgment, all of which are stated in Romans 2.

1. *Judgment is according to truth.*

The first principle: God's judgment is based on truth. It is based upon real facts, not hearsay.

> But we know that the judgment of God is according to truth against those who practice such things.
> Romans 2:2

Consider, for instance, when the Lord wanted to find out the truth about the condition of Sodom and Gomorrah. He had heard terrible reports from the angels and others, but He said to Abraham, "I've come down to see for Myself." (See Genesis 18:20–21.) God never judges by hearsay; He judges according to truth.

2. Judgment is according to deeds.

> [He] *"will render to each one according to his deeds."*
> *verse 6*

We will be judged for what we have done. That is a basic principle that runs through the Bible and it applies to believers as well as unbelievers. Peter unfolds this principle as well, applying it specifically to believers:

> And if you call on the Father, who without partiality judges
> according to each one's work, conduct yourselves throughout
> the time of your stay here in fear. . . .
> 1 Peter 1:17

This fact is not publicly disseminated in most churches today. Peter tells believers that we must bear in mind that we are going to be judged according to what we have done and that we are to live reverent, godly lives in view of this fact. We must not be rash, proud, or presumptuous—because one day we will have to answer to God for everything we say and do. Bear in mind, this passage is addressed to believers, not to unbelievers.

Revelation 20 tells us that in the final judgment, all people will be judged according to what was written in the books, because God keeps a record of every life. In the days of the New Testament, books were not like today's volumes. They were scrolls rolled up like a tape. I am inclined to think that in the judgment every one of us will be confronted with something like a video tape that projects the entire course of our life before us.

God was dealing with me at one point in my life when I was very sick. I earnestly sought God as to why I was not being healed. One night God woke me up at two a.m. and gave me a review of the life I had been leading. I was a generally well accepted preacher (though sometimes criticized) at about the same level as many other preachers who are comparatively well known. However, God showed me that in many ways I had been extremely carnal. I had not committed any gross sins like sexual immorality, drunkenness or the misappropriation of funds. But nevertheless, God showed me there were things in my past that were displeasing to Him.

He brought to me the Scripture in Malachi where God says, "Jacob I have loved; but Esau I have hated" (Malachi 1:2–3). Esau is a type of the carnal man. There are no gross sins recorded about Esau; he just was a carnally-minded man. God said, "I hate that!"

After nearly fifty years in the ministry, God showed me that there were things in my life that He hated. He showed me that I had been careless in some respects. Some of the scenes He showed me were in restaurants. You may not realize that God judges you in restaurants, but He does. Somebody once said, "All you Americans can talk about is food." I have also heard it said, "If you want to find out where the best restaurants are, ask a preacher."

I began to realize what it means to spend the time of our stay (or sojourning) in this life in fear—not slavish fear, but reverent awe, as before God who will judge everything we say and everything we do.

3. Judgment is with no respect of persons.

Romans 2:11 states the third principle of God's judgment, which is judgment without respect of persons:

> For there is no partiality with God.
> Romans 2:11

All the modern translations are worded this way because it is a modern phrase. However, the original King James Version says, "There is no respect of persons with God." It is a much more accurate translation, because partiality can be toward any kind of person.

For example, think of a weak, insignificant person—you can be very partial to that person. They are so weak you really want to help them, and do everything you can for them. However, "respect of persons" means we are not impressed by what people are in their natural selves.

A man may be a general, a president, or a bishop, but he does not get any special judgment from God. He is treated just like everybody else. That is what is meant by the phrase "no respect of persons." It is particularly aimed at people who occupy positions of prominence in the world today.

4. Judgment is according to the measure of light.

The forth principle of God's judgment is according to the measure of light.

> For as many as have sinned without law will also perish without law, and as many as have sinned in the law will be judged by the law.
> Romans 2:12

If you have the law, you will be judged by it. If you do not have the law, you will not be judged by it, but you will still be judged for what you have done based on what you knew.

This principle is also illustrated by Jesus in Matthew 11 when He spoke to some of the major cities of His day who had not responded to His preaching.

> Then He began to rebuke the cities in which most of His mighty works had been done, because they did not repent: "Woe to you, Chorazin! Woe to you, Bethsaida! For if the mighty works which were done in you had been done in Tyre and Sidon, they would have repented long ago in sackcloth and ashes. But I say to you, it will be more tolerable for Tyre

and Sidon in the day of judgment than for you."
Matthew 11:20–22

Jesus said it will be more tolerable for Tyre and Sidon in the day of judgment because they had less light. Bethsaida and Chorazin had the greatest light and they would be more severely judged. You and I will be judged according to the light that is available to us.

Generally speaking, for people in the English-speaking world, there is a greater measure of light available today than has ever been available to any previous generation in history. We have masses of Bibles, endless books, CDs, DVDs, and preachers. We are going to be judged by the light that has been made available to us. Bear in mind that God's standards of judgment for this generation will be the most severe because we have had the most light.

Jesus goes on in the next verse:

> *"And you, Capernaum, who are exalted to heaven, will be brought down to Hades; for if the mighty works which were done in you had been done in Sodom, it would have remained until this day. But I say to you that it shall be more tolerable for the land of Sodom in the day of judgment than for you."*
> *verses 23–24*

Judgment is according to light: the more light we have, the stricter will be our judgment. There probably has never been a generation of Christians that have had the measure of light available that we have today. That is going to be the standard of our judgment and it is a sobering thought.

5. Judgment includes secret thoughts and motives.

The fifth and final principle of God's judgment is found in Romans 2:

In the day when God will judge the secrets of men by Jesus
Christ, according to my gospel.
Romans 2:16

God is not only going to judge our open acts, He is going to judge our secret, innermost thoughts, motives and attitudes. God is very concerned about our motives. Two people may perform the same outward action, but their motives may be entirely different. When God judges them, He will take into account their motives.

MY NOTES

Study Questions

Before you start, pray for the Holy Spirit to give you a clear revelation of your life in relation to Christ's judgment seat.

1. What special insights did you gain from this lesson?

    ----

2. The Bible describes two kinds of judgment. What are they, and what is the difference? Give an example of both. (Read Exodus 20:4-6, Jeremiah 32:18, Psalm 103:17-18 and Ezekiel 18:1-4, 20 to help you find an answer.)

    ----

3. How are God's mercy and His judgment related, i.e. how can a merciful God be judging?

----

4. According to Derek Prince, the sin of idolatry is the greatest of all sins. Why is it such a severe sin? What examples of idolatry do you know from this current age?

----

5. Reflect/discuss: We are, in a sense, responsible for the blessing or curse of future generations. Does this influence the way you live today? Do our sins impact the eternal judgment of our (grand) children as well?

----

6. Read Hebrews 9:27. According to this Scripture, how would you respond to the popular (Hindu) concept of reincarnation, which states that after death, someone's soul returns to the physical realm in a new body?

----

7. Do you think judgment is alien to God's nature? How do you think most believers view God in relation to judgment?

----

8. Romans 2 gives key principles of God's judgment (see verses 2 and 6 and 11-12 and 16). What are they? To whom do they apply?

----

9. What does it mean to live your life in godly fear? (compare also 1 Peter 1:17). How does Derek Prince' example from Esau's life apply to your own situation?

SUMMARY

- Romans 2:1-16 highlights five specific principles of God's judgment telling us **how** we will be judged:
  - We will be judged according to truth (v. 1-2).
  - We will be judged according to deeds (v. 6, also compare 1 Peter 1:17 and Revelation 20:12).
  - Verse 11 says, "There is no partiality with God," or "no respect of persons with God" (KJV). This phrase is found 11 times throughout the Bible.
  - People will be judged according to the measure of light that they have received (v. 12). Also compare Matthew 11:20-24.
  - Judgment will include our secret thoughts and motives (v. 16).

MEDITATION

If we are truly believers
in Jesus, we will be
judged, but we will not be
condemned.

2

Successive Scenes of Judgment

As I understand the judgments of God as they are presented in the New Testament, there are going to be four major, successive scenes of judgment.

I. The Judgment Seat of Christ

The first will be before the judgment seat of Christ. The Greek word for "judgment seat" is *bema* which means a platform on which a Roman official sat to execute judgment. Pontius Pilate sat on his *bema* when Jesus appeared before him for judgment. The judgment seat of Christ will be an eternal judgment for believers only. Remember Peter's admonition:

> *And if you call on the Father, who without partiality judges according to each one's work, conduct yourselves throughout the time of your stay here in fear.*
> *1 Peter 1:17*

This verse is written to us as Christians. We call on the Father.

Later on, Peter says:

> *For the time has come for judgment to begin at the house of God; and if it begins with us first, what will be the end of those who do not obey the gospel of God?*
> *1 Peter 4:17*

Judgment always begins with the house of God, always with the people who have the most truth. When judgment starts, the first people to be judged will be the Christians, and we will have a special judgment.

> But why do you judge your brother? Or why do you show contempt for your brother? For we [Christians] shall all stand before the judgment seat of Christ [the bema]. For it is written: "As I live, says the Lord, every knee shall bow to Me, and every tongue shall confess to God." So then each of us shall give account of himself to God.
> Romans 14:10–12

There is only one person you must give account of—yourself. You will not have to give account of your spouse or your pastor, and you may waste a lot of time judging others when you should be judging yourself. The only person you are going to have to give account for is yourself.

Paul says that all of us, as Christians, will have to give account of ourselves to God, a theme which he returns to in 2 Corinthians:

> For we [Christians] must all appear before the judgment seat of Christ, that each one may receive the things done in the body, according to what he has done, whether good or bad.
> 2 Corinthians 5:10

The New King James Version says, "We must all appear," but the Greek says, "We must all be made manifest." Before Christ's judgment seat there will be no secrets. Everything will be totally exposed. Nothing will be hidden.

We will stand before the judgment seat of Christ to receive according to the way we have lived in the body. And there are only two categories of deeds: good or bad. There is nothing in between. Everything that is not good is bad. Jesus said very clearly, "He who is not with Me is against Me" (Matthew 12:30). There is no neutrality. Jesus has excluded it.

Many people in church are sitting on the fence, unwilling to make a commitment. They are not on one side, nor are they on the other. They are not doing good, but neither would they admit to doing bad. Sometimes I tell people, "When the Holy Spirit comes to a church, one of the first things He does is to electrify the fence! You have to jump off on one side or the other." That is why a lot of people don't welcome the Holy Spirit—because He abolishes their neutrality. There is no neutrality with the Holy Spirit.

There are five main features of the judgment seat of Christ:

1. It is individual; each one will answer for himself.
2. It is for the things done in the body; the way we have lived while we were in this body.
3. There are only two categories: good or bad. "All unrighteousness is sin" (1 John 5:17), anything that is not righteous is sinful. A third category of neutrality seems to have slipped into people's thinking and it deceives many. However, there is no neutrality.
4. This judgment is not for condemnation. This is very important. We are going to be judged, but we are not going to be condemned if we are true, sincere believers in Jesus.
5. This judgment is for assessment of service.

Some of you may be a little concerned about this judgment, because we often think of condemnation when we think of judgment. There are three Scriptures which may comfort you at this point. First, Jesus says:

> *"He who believes in Him* [the Son] *is not condemned;*
> *but he who does not believe is condemned already."*
> *John 3:18*

If we are truly believers in Jesus, we will be judged, but we will not be condemned. Jesus says again in the most emphatic way He can:

> *"Most assuredly, I say to you, he who hears My word and believes in Him who sent Me has everlasting life, and shall not come into judgment [or condemnation], but has passed from death into life."*
> *John 5:24*

Finally:

> *There is therefore now no condemnation for those who are in Christ Jesus.*
> *Romans 8:1*

We are not talking about a judgment of condemnation but a judgment that will assess the service we have offered to Jesus during our lifetime. This judgment is described clearly in 1 Corinthians 3, where Paul is speaking about building:

> *For no other foundation can anyone lay than that which is laid, which is Jesus Christ. Now if anyone builds on this foundation with gold, silver, precious stones, wood, hay, straw, each one's work will become clear; for the Day will declare it, because it will be revealed by fire; and the fire will test each one's work, of what sort it is. If anyone's work which he has built on it endures, he will receive a reward. If anyone's work is burned, he will suffer loss; but he himself will be saved, yet so as through fire.*
> *1 Corinthians 3:11–15*

The New International Version translates the last phrase, "Like one escaping from the flames." This passage is the essence of the judgment of Christians.

First, we must be built on the foundation of Jesus Christ; there is no other foundation. By building on the foundation of Jesus Christ we are not building upon our own works or our own righteousness, but upon the foundation of Jesus Christ and His righteousness.

Next, the value, or quality, of the service we have offered will be determined. Paul places the believers' works in one of two categories: gold, silver, precious stones; or wood, hay, stubble. Remember that things that are easy to acquire can be offered in large quantities: wood, hay and stubble, but they will all be burned up. The things that are valuable are not obtained in large quantities: gold, silver, precious stones. Some people assess the quantity of their service, but that is not the way God assesses it. God looks for quality.

I examine myself continually. Am I just producing wood, hay or stubble that will be burned up? Or am I producing something of eternal value? What a tragedy it would be, having worked all your life for something, piled it all up, to then see fire sweep through it in the day of judgment and finish it all off. There is nothing left, but you are as a naked soul that is spared, like one escaping through the flames. What a solemn thought!

How to Withstand the Fire

How might we assess our service for Christ to know whether or not it will stand the fire of judgment? I suggest three ways to assess your own service.

1. Motive

The only motive acceptable to God is: for God's glory. Much of what is done in the Church today is done by men and women for their own glory. It is my observation that the greatest problem in the Church today is personal ambition on the part of ministers. Who has the largest church, the longest mailing list, or the most miracles? That will all be burned up because it is the wrong motive. Paul says:

> *Therefore, whether you eat or drink, or whatever you do,*
> *do all to the glory of God.*
> *1 Corinthians 10:31*

There is only one acceptable motive for our service and that is the glory of God. Pause for a moment as you are reading this and consider what has been motivating you in your service for the Lord.

In Romans 12:1, Paul said we need to be renewed in our minds. The difference between the renewed mind and the unrenewed mind is clear: the unrenewed mind says, "What's in this for me?" The renewed mind says, "Will God get the glory?" It is a total change of motivation.

This same principle applies to marriage. Many marriages are unhappy because the people approach them with an unrenewed mind. The attitude of each spouse is, "What will I get out of this? Will it make me happy?" This is almost a certain recipe for an unhappy marriage.

The right motive is, "What can I give?" When a man and a woman come together with the intention of giving to one another, they will have a happy and successful marriage. The whole issue of motivation is far more important than most people realize.

2. Obedience

Second, if your work is to stand the test of fire, it must be done in obedience to the Word of God; it is the only acceptable basis. In Matthew 7, Jesus spoke very plainly about obedience.

> *"Not everyone who says to Me, 'Lord, Lord,' shall enter the kingdom*
> *of heaven, but he who does the will of My Father in heaven."*
> *Matthew 7:21*

The only acceptable motive is to do the will of God the Father.

Then Jesus goes on with a statement that offends some people:

> *"Many will say to Me in that day, 'Lord, Lord, have we not prophesied in Your name, cast out demons in Your name, and done many wonders in Your name?' And then I will declare to them, 'I never knew you; depart from Me, you who practice lawlessness!'"*
> *verses 22–23*

By the grace of God, I have been privileged to cast out many demons. I have seen a number of very definite miracles take place. Frequently, I have prophesied. However, I do not base my hope of reward on any of that, and anybody who does is in danger. There is only one essential requirement for reward in heaven. It is doing the will of the Father who is in heaven. Jesus says to these miracle workers, "Depart from Me, you who practice lawlessness!"

In reality, many miracle workers are a law to themselves. They do basically whatever they feel like, take whatever they can get, and ignore the great central principles of the Word of God.

Jesus concludes His sermon in Matthew 7 with these words:

> *"Therefore whoever hears these sayings of Mine, and does them, I will liken him to a wise man who built his house on the rock: and the rain descended, the floods came, and the winds blew and beat on that house; and it did not fall, for it was founded on the rock. But everyone who hears these sayings of Mine, and does not do them, will be like a foolish man who built his house on the sand: and the rain descended, the floods came, and the winds blew and beat on that house; and it fell. And great was its fall."*
> *verses 24–27*

The difference between the man who built upon the rock and the one who built upon the sand is clearly stated by Jesus. It is the one who does not merely hear His words, but also "does them."

I once wrote a teaching letter about Balaam because I was so impressed with his story. Here was a man with miraculous prophetic gifts, words of knowledge and words of wisdom. In Numbers 22–24, he gave forth prophecies as beautiful as any that are uttered in the Bible concerning the destiny of Israel. Yet he perished. He was executed by the people of Israel. Do you know what Balaam's problem was? He is mentioned three times in the New Testament, and each mention states very clearly that Balaam's motivation was love of money. That cost him his soul.

Second Corinthians 2:17 says, "Unlike so many, we do not peddle the word of God for profit" (NIV). That is a startling statement Paul made concerning the time in which he lived. Paul said there were many people motivated by making profit out of the gospel.

In today's Church, we need to ask ourselves if we are motivated by the love of money or if we are motivated by the glory of God and obedience to His Word. It is our motives and obedience that God searches.

3. In the Power of the Holy Spirit

The third way of assessing our service is the power in which we operate. Paul says:

> For I will not dare to speak of any of those things which Christ
> has not accomplished through me, in word and deed,
> to make the Gentiles obedient—in mighty signs and wonders,
> by the power of the Spirit of God.
> Romans 15:18–19

Paul says that there is nothing he ever did that is worth mentioning except that which the Holy Spirit had done through him.

That is the only acceptable power for ministry—the power of the Holy Spirit. Too much of what is accomplished today in the Church is the product of human, fleshly effort. As good as that may appear, it will not ultimately stand up under the judgment of Christ.

There are, then, three requirements for our work to stand the test of fire.

1. What is our motive? Is it for God's glory?
2. Are we working in obedience to the Word of God? Or are we doing our own thing or making our own rules?
3. Are we working in the power of the Holy Spirit or in our own fleshly ability?

Two Patterns of Judgment

There are two fundamental patterns of judgment for believers that Jesus related in two different parables—one based on ability, the other on percentage. The first is the Parable of the Minas found in Luke 19. (A mina is a measurement of money.)

> *Now as they heard these things, He spoke another parable, because He was near Jerusalem and because they thought the kingdom of God would appear immediately. Therefore He said: "A certain nobleman went into a far country to receive for himself a kingdom and to return.* [It was going to be a long while before he got back.] *So he called ten of his servants, delivered to them ten minas* [one each] *and said to them, ' Do business till I come.'* [In other words, make a profit.] *But his citizens hated him, and sent a delegation after him, saying, 'We will not have this man to reign over us.' And so it was*

that when he returned, having received the kingdom,
he then commanded these servants, to whom he had given
the money, to be called to him, that he might know how much
every man had gained by trading."
Luke 19:11–15

God is going to require an accounting of service from each one of us, and our faithfulness in service in this life will determine the position we occupy in eternity—that is, the responsibility we will be able to carry in the kingdom of God.

"Then came the first, saying, 'Master, your mina has earned
ten minas.' And he said to him, 'Well done, good servant;
because you were faithful in a very little, have authority over
ten cities.' And the second came, saying, 'Master, your mina
has earned five minas.' Likewise he said to him, 'You also be
over five cities.'"
verses 16–19

Notice the master didn't say, "Well done, good servant." This was a little lower level of commendation.

"Then another [the third] came, saying, 'Master, here is your
mina, which I have kept put away in a handkerchief. For I
feared you, because you are an austere man. You collect
what you did not deposit, and reap what you did not sow.'
And he said to him, 'Out of your own mouth I will judge you,
you wicked servant. You knew that I was an austere man,
collecting what I did not deposit and reaping what I did not
sow. Why then did you not put my money in the bank, that
at my coming I might have collected it with interest?' And he
said to those who stood by, 'Take the mina from him, and give
it to him who has ten minas.' (But they said to him, 'Master,
he has ten minas.')"
verses 20–25

The bystanders really did not think it was right that the one who already had ten should get one more. But Jesus goes on:

> "'For I say to you, that to everyone who has will be given; and from him who does not have, even what he has will be taken away from him.'"
> verse 26

Pay careful attention to this, because most of us do not think the way Jesus thinks. He gave to the one who had ten minas because that servant had proven he could be faithful with whatever was entrusted to him. The first servant made the most and was rewarded with the most. This is a principle of multiplying what we have been given.

Use It or Lose It

At one time, God gave me a supernatural gift of faith in a very strange way. I would pray for people with unequal legs and the short leg would grow out. It happened to literally hundreds of people and as it did I would tell them, "Now, God has touched you. His supernatural power is working in your body; help yourself to all that God is giving you." As a result, many people were supernaturally healed of a multitude of ailments.

However, some of my fellow ministers said, "You know, Derek, you have a reputation as a dignified Bible teacher. If you go around holding people's feet and lengthening their legs, it may not fit in with your reputation."

So I thought, "Maybe they're right."

I questioned the Lord about the matter and this is what I believe He said: I've given you a gift. I suddenly realized it was a gift, the gift of faith.

Then I believe the Lord explained, There are two things you can do. You can use it and get more, or you can fail to use it and lose it. I made up my mind at that point I was going to use it and get more. I have to say, to the glory of God, I believe I received more.

Whatever gift you have been given, there are two things you can do: You can use it and receive more, or you can fail to use it and lose it.

Laboring Faithfully

Second, as we have already seen, your service in this life will determine your position in eternity. The one who gained ten minas was given authority over ten cities, and the one who gained five minas was placed over five cities. Their position in eternity was in exact proportion to their faithfulness in this life.

Notice, Jesus did not say, "Well done, good and successful servant," He said, "Well done, good and faithful servant." Some of us put too much emphasis on success and too little emphasis on faithfulness.

I have been privileged to see tremendous works of God in many foreign mission fields. I could get a little puffed up and say, "Isn't that wonderful! Thousands of people come to my seminars." However, God has reminded me, "Don't forget, there was a generation before you that saw very little fruit. They labored faithfully and you have entered into their labors. Don't give yourself too much credit for this fruit."

I respect the pioneers: the men and women who labored and laid down their lives. When the first missionaries went to East Africa, four out of every five died before they had been there many months. They saw few results for their brief labor. However, their lives were seeds planted in the earth that brought forth fruit later on. Though many of them saw very little fruit, they were faithful to the work God sent them to do. That faithfulness, I believe, has earned them great reward in heaven.

Put It in the Bank

The third man in the Parable of the Minas produced no return on the money entrusted to him. His master said to him, "Well, you maybe didn't have the ability to make money yourself, but you could have put it in the bank. Then I would have gotten my own with interest."

How does that apply to us? What could we do if we feel we are not extremely gifted people? We might think, "I don't have a big ministry; I'm not a preacher or an administrator. What can I do?" We can "put it in the bank." We can find a ministry that is bringing forth fruit, examine the ministry to see if it is genuine, and then invest in it. You may invest your money or you may invest some of your time. This is a legitimate way of multiplying what God has given you. This is putting the money in the bank. We will receive our reward when the Lord comes.

Jesus as Judge

At the end of the Parable of the Minas the master declares:

> *"'But bring here those enemies of mine, who did not want me to reign over them, and slay them before me.'"*
> *verse 27*

This parable is a picture of Jesus as the Judge. Here Jesus is not the Savior; but Jesus the Judge. Remember, the same person who is the Savior is also the Judge, and as thorough and efficient as He is in saving, so He will be in judging.

Does your picture of Jesus include that? Or are you one of those who say, "Gentle Jesus, meek and mild"? Praise God, that is true also, but it is not the whole truth. There is another side to Jesus. He is the Judge with eyes like a flame of fire, a two-edged sword that goes out of His mouth, a voice like the sound of many waters, feet like bronze refined in a furnace. (See Revelation 1:12–16.)

When John the Revelator met Him in that capacity, he fell at His feet as one dead. That impresses me! This is John—the one who had the closest relationship of all the disciples with Jesus. He had lain on the bosom of Jesus at the Last Supper. He had been one of those who was at the Sea of Galilee when Jesus had revealed Himself after His resurrection and made breakfast for them. (I like the fact that Jesus had breakfast ready for His disciples.)

However, when John, who has known Jesus so intimately, is confronted by Jesus the Judge, he falls at His feet like one dead.

I think something like that needs to happen to the Church in our day. The Church, which has been living on a buddy-buddy relationship with Jesus, needs to be confronted by Jesus the Judge.

It certainly would not do us any harm if we fell at His feet like someone dead.

The Parable of the Talents

The second pattern for the judgment of our service is found in the Parable of the Talents in Matthew:

> *"For the kingdom of heaven is like a man traveling to a far country, who called his own servants and delivered his goods to them. And to one he gave five talents, to another two, and to another one, to each according to his own ability; and immediately he went on a journey."*
> *Matthew 25:14–15*

In the Parable of the Minas, each servant received one mina but in this parable one servant received five talents, one received two, and one received one. The talents (like the minas) are a sum of money. They were distributed to the servants according to their ability. God gives us talents according to what He knows we can do with them.

If you can use five talents, He will give you five. If you can only use two, He will give you two. And, if you can only use one, He will give you one. According to your ability He measures what He gives.

> "Then he who had received the five talents went and traded with them, and made another five talents. And likewise, he who had received two gained two more also. But he who had received one went and dug in the ground, and hid his lord's money. After a long time the lord of those servants came and settled accounts with them."
> verses 16–19

We need to keep in mind that the Lord is going to come and settle accounts with us.

> "So he who had received five talents came and brought five other talents, saying, 'Lord, you delivered to me five talents; look, I have gained five more talents besides them.' His lord said to him, 'Well done, good and faithful servant; you were faithful over a few things, I will make you ruler over many things. Enter into the joy of your lord.'"
> verses 20–21

Notice the same principle as in the previous parable: what you do in this world will determine what you do in eternity.

> "He also who had received two talents came and said, ' Lord, you delivered to me two talents; look, I have gained two more talents besides them.'His lord said to him, 'Well done, good and faithful servant; you have been faithful over a few

things, I will make you ruler over many things. Enter into the
joy of your lord.'"
verses 22–23

In this parable there is a different principle of commendation. One servant made five talents and the other made two, but the words of commendation were exactly the same to each of them. In other words, it is the percentage God looks for. If you have received five, He expects a hundred percent; five more. If you received two, He also expects a hundred percent; two more. He knows what you are capable of, and He asks no more from you than He knows you can deliver.

"Then he who had received the one talent came and said,
'Lord, I knew you to be a hard man, reaping where you have
not sown, and gathering where you have not scattered seed.
And I was afraid, and went and hid your talent in the ground.
Look, there you have what is yours.' But his lord answered
and said to him, 'You wicked and lazy servant.'"
verses 24–26

Please note that laziness is wickedness. Most of our churches would not accept drunkards as part of the congregation. However, many of our churches would accept lazy people. In the sight of God, I think laziness is a worse sin than drunkenness. That is the way I see Jesus measuring things. Please understand, I do not endorse drunkenness—it is a sin. However, I think in the eyes of God laziness is a worse sin. Jesus said:

"You wicked and lazy servant, you knew that I reap where I
have not sown, and gather where I have not scattered seed.
So you ought to have deposited my money with the bankers,
and at my coming I would have received back my own with
interest.'"
verses 26–27

Again we see the same "investment" principle as in the previous parable. If you do not have the ability to produce fruit yourself, invest it in a ministry that is bringing forth fruit.

> "Therefore take the talent from him, and give it to him who has ten talents. [The one who has, receives more.] For to everyone who has, more will be given, and he will have abundance; but from him who does not have, even what he has will be taken away. And cast the unprofitable servant into the outer darkness. There will be weeping and gnashing of teeth."
> verses 28–30

That phrase "weeping and gnashing of teeth" is used several times in the New Testament. I have studied where it is used and have come to the conclusion that it is only used about people who have been very close to the real thing in God and missed out. They had every opportunity, but failed to apprehend what God had for them.

A Serious Lesson

This is not written about people who never knew anything about God. It is the people who have been right on the edge of God's best all their lives but never entered in. Those are the ones of whom the Bible says, "There will be weeping and gnashing of teeth." They will have tremendous bitterness, saying, "I could have been in this. I had the opportunity all the time but I never availed myself of it. Now I'm cast out forever into outer darkness." This should motivate us to fearlessly pursue the things of God.

Furthermore, the people in this parable who were rejected were the ones who had the least committed to them, the one-talent people. I find in most churches that the people who have great ability will do something with it. However, the one-talent people sit back and say, "There is nothing much I can do, so I won't do anything." They are the ones who are in danger of being rejected; they will be cast out.

I would say to the one-talent persons that most of you have underestimated your responsibilities. You have said, "I don't have much; there's not much I can do. God doesn't require much of me." God does. He requires faithfulness, whether you have a little or whether you have much.

I once preached on this in my own church in Fort Lauderdale, Florida. Talking to the one-talent people, I asked for a response from those who felt they had one talent and had not been using their talent. The response was shocking. About half the congregation responded when I asked them to stand for prayer! I came to see this as a major problem with many believers.

It is too easy to simply say, "I've only one talent, so what can I do with it? I'll do nothing." Jesus will not accept that as an excuse. He would say, "You can put it in the bank. You can invest your one talent in a ministry that is really bringing forth fruit. Then much of that fruit will be credited to you."

Dear one-talent person, look out! You are in danger. You may one day hear the words, "Cast the unprofitable servant into outer darkness. There will be weeping and gnashing of teeth."

Sober Assessments

Here are three conclusions we may draw from the study of these parables:

1. Our service in this life determines our position in the next life.
2. Not to use your talent is to lose it.
3. Not to do good when you can is sin. James 4:17 says, "Therefore, to him who knows to do good and does not do it, to him it is sin."

Sins of omission are just as real as the sins of commission. In Matthew 25, three classes of people were totally rejected by God. The foolish virgins who took no oil (verse 12), the one-talent servant who did nothing with his talent (verse 30), and the goat nations who did not help the brothers of Jesus (verse 46). They were all totally and finally rejected by God.

I asked myself one day, "What did they all have in common that caused them to be rejected? What did they do?" I got a simple answer, "They did nothing." That is all you have to do to be rejected—nothing. It is a solemn thought.

MY NOTES

Study Questions

1. What was new or stood out for you from this lesson?

   ----

2. Where does judgment begin? Why?

   ----

3. Reflect/discuss: if we are truly believers in Jesus, we will be judged, but we will not be condemned. All your work will be made manifest. (see 1 Corinthians 3:11-15 and Hebrews 9:27) Write down any thoughts and questions this raises with you and turn them

into a prayer to God. Consider how to incorporate thanksgiving into your prayer.

---

4. The first major scene of judgment will be the judgment of Christian believers before the Judgment Seat of Christ (Compare 1 Peter 4:17, Romans 14:10-12 and 2 Corinthians 5:10). List five key features of this judgment.

---

5. Derek Prince stated, that our actions fit into only two categories - good or bad. There is nothing in between. Everything that is not good is bad. Would you agree or not?

---

6. Respond: sins of omission are no less serious than those of commission.

----

7. What is the difference between a renewed mind and an unrenewed mind? How can you develop a renewed mind?

----

8. Reflect/discuss: our service in this life determines our position in the next life.

----

9. Jesus told two similar stories about the Minas (Luke 19:11-27) and the Talents (Matthew 25:14-30) as patterns for judgment. Both servants who did nothing were totally rejected. All they had to do to be rejected was **nothing** – a very solemn thought. Write down any thoughts or questions you have. Turn it into prayer afterwards.

----

10. In this parable, how does Derek Prince interpret the meaning of putting your money in the bank?

----

11. List the things that the Lord has given to you which can be profitably used for His kingdom. Do you feel you are using each of them to the best of your ability? What could you do to increase them? Why would you want to – what is your motive?

----

12. What is the mistake people make when they reason: "I don't have many talents, there is not much I can do. God doesn't require much of me."

SUMMARY

- The first major scene of judgment will the judgment of Christian believers before the Judgment Seat of Christ. (1 Peter 4:17, Romans 14:10-12 and 2 Corinthians 5:10.)
    - It is a personal judgment of individuals (2 Corinthians 5:10).
    - It relates to things done in the body. There are only two categories: good or bad. (2 Corinthians 5:10)
    - It is not for condemnation (see John 3:18, John 5:24 and Romans 8:1). It is for the assessment of our service (1 Corinthians 3:11-15).

- The Bible reveals three requirements which we have to meet if we are to stand up to the fire:
    - Our motives have to be correct – we need to be seeking God's glory (1 Corinthians 10:31).
    - We need to be obedient to God's Word (Matthew 7:21-27).
    - We must live in the power of the Holy Spirit (Romans 15:18-19).

- Our service in this life determines our position in the next life.
- Not to use the gifts that God gives us means that we will ultimately lose them (Luke 19:26).

MY NOTES

I believe a person can get to heaven without theology. But I doubt whether a person will ever get to heaven without courage.

3

Three other Judgments

I The Judgment of Israel

Up to now we have been dealing with the judgment of believers, because that is the one that really concerns each of us. However, there are three other judgments to take place.

The next judgment is a judgment in history—the judgment of Israel, a special people set apart by God. Though the Jews as a whole have been disobedient and unfaithful for many centuries, God has never permanently rejected them. The Scripture says:

> *"The Lord will not forsake His people, for His great name's sake, because it has pleased the Lord to make you [Israel] His people."*
> *1 Samuel 12:22*

God's faithfulness to Israel is not because Israel deserves it, but because of God's name, that it may be glorified. God is going to deal with Israel in a special way. Here is a principle that I want to pass on to you about blessing and judgment: God blesses the Jews directly, but He blesses the Gentiles through the Jews. However, God judges the Gentiles directly, but He judges the Jews through the Gentiles.

Those of us who are Gentiles need to remember that every spiritual blessing we have ever received we owe to the Jewish people. Jesus said in John 4:22, "Salvation is of the Jews." Every single blessing we have ever received in salvation we owe to one people—the Jewish people. God expects us, as Gentiles, to recognize that and act accordingly. (See Romans 11:17–22.) When it comes to judgment, God judges the Gentiles directly.

But He judges the Jews through the Gentiles. Through hundreds of years of Jewish history God has persistently used Gentile nations to judge the Jews for their disobedience and their unfaithfulness. The final judgment of Israel will take place during the Great Tribulation. Consider Jeremiah's prophecy concerning this time:

> "'For behold, the days are coming,' says the Lord, 'that I will bring back from captivity [exile] My people Israel and Judah," says the Lord. 'And I will cause them to return to the land that I gave to their fathers, and they shall possess it.'"
> Jeremiah 30:3

No matter what any government or politician thinks, the Bible says, "they shall possess it." Everybody who knows the Bible knows "the land" is the little piece of land which is today called Israel.

A preacher friend of mine once said, "If the return of the Jews to their land was from God, there would be peace." However, he did not know his Bible, because God says in connection with the return of the Jews:

> These are the words that the Lord spoke concerning Israel and Judah. "For thus says the Lord: 'We have heard a voice of trembling, of fear, and not of peace. Ask now, and see, whether a man is ever in labor with child? So why do I see every man with his hands on his loins like a woman in labor, and all faces turned pale?'"
> verses 4–6

The greatest pressure that Israel has ever experienced is immediately ahead, after they have returned to the land.

> *"Alas! For that day is great, so that none is like it; and it is the time of Jacob's trouble, but he shall be saved out of it."*
> *verse 7*

Notice, it does not say saved from it, but saved out of it. There God will deal in judgment with the Jewish people. At the end of the Tribulation, their judgment will have taken place.

II The Judgment of the gentile nations

Following the judgment of Israel, God will judge the other nations. This judgment takes place at the end of the Tribulation just before the beginning of the Millennium.

> *"For behold, in those days and at that time, when I bring back the captives* [exiles] *of Judah and Jerusalem,* [Notice this refers to the same period—the return of the Jewish people to their own land. God says:] *I will also gather all nations* [Gentile nations], *and bring them down to the Valley of Jehoshaphat; and I will enter into judgment with them there on account of My people, My heritage Israel, whom they have scattered among the nations; they have also divided up My land."*
> *Joel 3:1–2*

God says that when He has finished dealing with the Jews, He will then deal with the Gentiles. He will deal with them on one basis—the way they have treated Israel. That is a remarkable fact, but there it is.

In the passage above, God has two accusations against the Gentile nations: first, they have oppressed the Jewish people; and second, they have divided up (or partitioned) the land. God says, "That's My land. I gave it to Israel, and no human authority or government has any right whatever to divide that land up."

What is happening today? Exactly what God said should not happen. The land has been partitioned, is being partitioned and probably will be partitioned. However, when God comes in judgment, He will judge the nations that have partitioned that land. Unfortunately, He could put Britain at the top of the list, because Britain was responsible for a major partitioning of the land. At the end of World War I the British were authorized to provide a national home for the Jewish people in what was then a large area known as Palestine. In the year 1922, by a single decision of Winston Churchill, Britain allocated seventy-six percent of that land to an Arab nation, which is now called Jordan, where no Jew was permitted to live. The remaining twenty-four percent of land has been divided by the United Nations. All of these Gentile nations are going to have to answer to Jesus for these acts when He comes. Regarding the judgment of the nations, we read in Matthew 25:32–46 that Jesus separates the nations into two groups: the sheep and the goats. The sheep nations are invited into the kingdom; the goat nations are dismissed from the kingdom and sent into everlasting punishment. The basic principle of division is the way they have treated the brothers of Jesus. This is so important because Israel is a major factor in world affairs today and many of the nations are lining up on the wrong side. Israel cannot defend itself; but, sooner or later, when the time comes, God will intervene.

III The Great White Throne Judgment

The fourth judgment is before the Great White Throne which is described in Revelation 20. This great eternal judgment is a judgment of all unbelievers. John the Revelator paints a most awesome and vivid picture of what this final and great judgment will be like. Revelation 20:11–15:

Then I saw a great white throne and Him who sat on it,
from whose face the earth and the heaven fled away.
And there was found no place for them.
verse 11

Think how terrible to appear before the One from whom earth and heaven have to flee, when He is in His majesty and in His wrath against sinners. John continues:

And I saw the dead, the small and great, standing before
God, and books were opened. And another book was opened,
which is the Book of Life. And the dead were judged according
to their works, by the things which were written in the books.
verse 12

In other words, the book contains the records of all they had done in this life; and this was the most complete and universal judgment. All human beings from every corner of this earth were assembled before this throne. This is how John describes it:

The sea gave up the dead who were in it, and Death and
Hades [Sheol, the place of departed spirits] *delivered up the*
dead who were in them. And they were judged, each one
according to his works. Then Death and Hades were cast into
the lake of fire. This is the second death.
verses 13–14

Remember that the second death is the irrevocable, eternal banishment from the presence of Almighty God, but it is not cessation of consciousness. Once we become beings, consciousness continues forever and ever. And then John sums it up this way:

And anyone not found written in the Book of Life was cast
into the lake of fire.
verse 15

Held to Account

We need to note some important facts from this passage. First, even after resurrection, these individuals are still called "the dead." John says, "I saw the dead, the small and great, standing before God."

Their bodies had been restored to them, but they were still dead. Dead in trespasses and sins; alienated and cut off from the life of God; and resurrected in their bodies to receive judgment for what they had done in their bodies.

Second, there are universal records kept of everything that each one of us has ever done. All has been recorded. There will be universal accountability, each one being required to answer for what they have done.

The word accountability is most unpleasant in the ears of modern culture. There are many different religions and philosophies today whose supreme objective is to declare to man that he is not really accountable to anybody but himself. I want to serve notice on you, that is a lie! Man is accountable to his Creator, who will one day be his judge. All of us are accountable.

Finally, there is only one way of escape from this judgment: through the Book of Life. Everyone whose name was not written in the Book of Life was thrown into the lake of fire.

Now who, or what kind of person, has his name written in the Book of Life? In Revelation 21:7, John goes on to describe the kind of person whose name is written in the Book of Life. Jesus says:

> *"He who overcomes shall inherit all things* [all the glories of heaven], *and I will be his God and he shall be My son."*

Notice, the primary requirement is to overcome; not to be defeated by sin and by the world and by ungodliness and by Satan. "He who overcomes shall inherit all things, and I will be his God and he shall be My son."

John defines overcoming in his first epistle:

For whatever is born of God overcomes the world. And this is the victory that has overcome the world— our faith. Who is he who overcomes the world, but he who believes that Jesus is the Son of God?
1 John 5:4–5

The requirement is to be born of God through faith. What are we required to believe? That Jesus is the Son of God. He who believes that Jesus is the Son of God and is born again through that faith, has the faith to overcome the world. That overcoming faith will cause him to inherit all things. God will be his God and he will be the son of God.

The alternative is stated in Revelation 21:8, where John describes the kind of person who will be thrown into the lake of fire:

"But the cowardly, unbelieving, abominable, murderers, sexually immoral, sorcerers, idolaters, and all liars shall have their part in the lake which burns with fire and brimstone, which is the second death."

It is easy for us to understand that immoral persons and murderers and sorcerers and liars will be be in the lake of fire. But would you note that the first two in the list are the cowardly and unbelieving? Those are the first two categories of people who are lost.

I believe a person can get to heaven without theology. But I doubt whether a person will ever get to heaven without courage. In the midst of an unbelieving world it takes courage to believe Jesus is the Son of God and remain faithful to Him.

The Great Divide

I was once visiting the Rocky Mountains in the state of Colorado. Someone pointed a little west of where we stood and said, "That ridge is the watershed of the continental United States. The rain that falls on one side flows down into the Pacific Ocean and the rain that falls on the other side ultimately flows down into the Gulf of Mexico."

I realized that even though there might only be a few inches between where two raindrops fell, their ultimate destiny was thousands of miles apart. As I was picturing that in my mind, I said to myself, Jesus is the watershed of human souls. Their destiny in eternity is determined by which side of Jesus they are on.

Two souls can be so close together—husband and wife, parent and child, or brother and sister—yet one is on one side of Jesus, having received Him and believed in Him. The other is on the other side, not having believed and not having received.

Though they are so close in this life, their ultimate destiny is an immeasurable distance apart. One will end in the eternal glory of heaven and the other will end in the lake of fire, the place of eternal judgment and destiny for unbelievers.

The tiny little difference of a few inches in where two raindrops fall in the Rockies determines their ultimate destination.

So it is with you and me. Just a tiny little difference in this life— one side of Jesus or the other—will determine our eternal destiny.

The four main judgments, then, are:

1. The judgment seat of Christ, a judgment of believers only.
2. The judgment of Israel in the Great Tribulation.

3. The judgment of all other nations before Christ's throne at the beginning of the Millennium.
4. The final judgment of all the remaining dead before the Great White Throne.

Am I Prepared?

Those are the principles of God's judgment as I understand them. You now need to ask yourself, "Am I prepared to face the judgment of God? Am I living the kind of life that will not cause me to be ashamed when I stand before Him?"

Now that you have read this book, I offer this prayer, if you would like to pray it for yourself:

PRAYER

Almighty God, Your Word is so clear. I pray that these words, taken directly from the Bible, will sink deep into my heart, and that they will prompt me to seriously examine my own life.

I pray especially for myself as a one-talent person. Lord, don't let me hide that talent in the ground. Help me to deposit it with the bankers that I may not be ashamed before You when You come.

Lord Jesus, You have spoken to us many times that You are coming quickly, You are coming soon. You have warned us many times that we need to be ready for Your coming.

I pray that You would grant me, by Your grace, to be ready for Your return, to be ready to stand before the judgment seat of Jesus and give an answer to the things I have done in the body. Lord, I pray for mercy, in Your name—the name of Jesus. Amen.

Study Questions

1. What special insights did you gain from this lesson?

   ----

2. List the four major, successive scenes of judgment that you have now studied.

   ----

3. Read Joel 3:1-2. What two accusations does God have against the Gentile nations? What does this passage have to do with Jerusalem today? How does this passage relate to the politics of your own country?

----

4. Pray for all politicians (globally and in your own country) who are involved in drafting resolutions and plans regarding Israel to receive God's wisdom and act according God's plan.

----

5. Reflect/discuss: Those of us who are believers from the Gentiles (non-Jewish nations) need to remember that every spiritual blessing we have ever received we owe to the Jewish people. What implications does this have for your attitude towards them? Think of ways you can return the blessing to the Jewish people.

----

6. Revelation 20:11-15 speaks about 'the dead' being judged. What does it imply that they are still called 'the dead' even though their bodies had been restored to them? How will they be judged?

----

7. Considering all that you have learned about God's judgment, what are some of the false ideas mankind has developed about judgment?

----

8. Do you think your country is in danger of God's judgment? If so, why? What about the Church in your country; is it in danger of God's judgment? How might these judgments be avoided?

----

9. This solemn study about God's eternal judgment is listed in Hebrews 6 as part of the basic Christian doctrines. Why do you think the Holy Spirit chose to place eternal judgment among the foundational doctrines of faith in Hebrews 6?

    ----

10. Why do you think our comprehension of the finality and terribleness of the judgment of the Lake of Fire is so shallow?

    ----

11. Ask yourself, "Am I prepared to face the judgment of God? Am I living the kind of life that will not cause me to be ashamed when I stand before Him?"

    Below you will find the prayer that Derek prayed at the end of his teaching on the final judgment, but it has been personalized, so for example, when Derek says, "Lord, don't let **them** hide", you can pray "Lord, don't let **me** hide."

Lord, don't let me hide my one talent in the ground. Help me to deposit it with the bankers that I may not be ashamed before You when You come. Lord Jesus, You have spoken to me many times that You are coming quickly; You are coming soon. You've warned me many times even through these studies that I need to be ready for Your coming.

Grant me by Your grace to be ready for Your return, to be ready to stand before the judgment seat of Jesus and give an answer to the things I've done in the body. Lord, I pray this mercy in Your Name, the Name of Jesus. Amen.

SUMMARY

- God blesses Israel directly but the Gentiles through the Jews. God judges the Gentiles directly but the Jews through the Gentiles.

- No matter what any government or politician thinks, Israel is going to possess the land that God gave to Abraham, Isaac and Jacob.

- In Matthew 25:31-46, we read about Jesus coming to judge the nations:
  - The 'sheep' nations are invited into the Kingdom.
  - The 'goats' nations are sent into everlasting punishment. The basic principle of division is the way they have treated the brothers of Jesus: the Jewish people.

- The fourth and last judgment takes place before the great white throne referred to in Revelation 20:11-15. The dead, great and small will be judged by what is written of their lives in the books.

- We thank God that there's another book which is the Book of Life. Those whose names are written in the Book of Life will enter into eternity with God. The rest will be banished forever from the presence of God.

This study was the tenth and final part of the Foundations – Faith Live Essentials series. You can find more information about the other titles in this series in the back of this book or visit www.dpmuk.org/foundations.

SCRIPTURES TO MEMORIZE

*Recall and write down the verses you memorized
at the beginning of this book:*

2 Corinthians 5:10

----

1 Peter 1:17

About the Author

Derek Prince (1915–2003) was born in India of British parents. He was educated as a scholar of Greek and Latin at Eton College and King's College, Cambridge in England. Upon graduation he held a fellowship (equivalent to a professorship) in Ancient and Modern Philosophy at King's College. Prince also studied Hebrew, Aramaic, and modern languages at Cambridge and the Hebrew University in Jerusalem. As a student, he was a philosopher and self-proclaimed agnostic.

Bible Teacher

While in the British Medical Corps during World War II, Prince began to study the Bible as a philosophical work. Converted through a powerful encounter with Jesus Christ, he was baptized in the Holy Spirit a few days later. Out of this encounter, he formed two conclusions: first, that Jesus Christ is alive; second, that the Bible is a true, relevant, up-to-date book. These conclusions altered the whole course of his life, which he then devoted to studying and teaching the Bible as the Word of God.

Discharged from the army in Jerusalem in 1945, he married Lydia Christensen, founder of a children's home there. Upon their marriage, he immediately became father to Lydia's eight adopted daughters – six Jewish, one Palestinian Arab, and one English. Together, the family saw the rebirth of the state of Israel in 1948. In the late 1950s, they adopted another daughter while Prince was serving as principal of a teacher training college in Kenya.

In 1963, the Princes immigrated to the United States and pastored a church in Seattle. In 1973, Prince became one of the founders of Intercessors for America. His book Shaping History through Prayer and

Fasting has awakened Christians around the world to their responsibility to pray for their governments. Many consider underground translations of the book as instrumental in the fall of communist regimes in the USSR, East Germany, and Czechoslovakia.

Lydia Prince died in 1975, and Prince married Ruth Baker (a single mother to three adopted children) in 1978. He met his second wife, like his first wife, while she was serving the Lord in Jerusalem. Ruth died in December 1998 in Jerusalem, where they had lived since 1981.

Teaching, Preaching and Broadcasting

Until a few years before his own death in 2003 at the age of eighty-eight, Prince persisted in the ministry God had called him to as he traveled the world, imparting God's revealed truth, praying for the sick and afflicted, and sharing his prophetic insights into world events in the light of Scripture. Internationally recognized as a Bible scholar and spiritual patriarch, Derek Prince established a teaching ministry that spanned six continents and more than sixty years.

He is the author of more than fifty books, six hundred audio teachings, and one hundred video teachings, many of which have been translated and published in more than one hundred languages.

He pioneered teaching on such groundbreaking themes as generational curses, the biblical significance of Israel, and demonology. Prince's radio program, which began in 1979, has been translated into more than a dozen languages and continues to touch lives. Derek's main gift of explaining the Bible and its teaching in a clear and simple way has helped build a foundation of faith in millions of lives. His nondenominational, nonsectarian approach has made his teaching equally relevant and helpful to people from all racial and religious backgrounds, and his teaching is estimated to have reached more than half the globe.

DPM Worldwide Ministry

In 2002, he said, "It is my desire – and I believe the Lord's desire – that this ministry continue the work, which God began through me over sixty years ago, until Jesus returns." Derek Prince Ministries International continues to reach out to believers in over 140 countries with Derek's teaching, fulfilling the mandate to keep on "until Jesus returns." This is accomplished through the outreaches of more than thirty Derek Prince offices around the world, including primary work in Australia, Canada, China, France, Germany, the Netherlands, New Zealand, Norway, Russia, South Africa, Switzerland, the United Kingdom, and the United States.

For current information about these and other worldwide locations, visit **www.derekprince.com.**

FOUNDATIONS
faith life essentials

www.dpmuk.org/shop

This book is part of a series of 10 studies on the foundations of the Christian faith.

Order the other books to get everything you need to develop a strong, balanced, Spirit-filled life!

1. Founded on the Rock
There is only one foundation strong enough for the Christian life, and we must be sure our lives are built on Jesus Himself.

2. Authority and Power of God's Word

Both the Bible and Jesus Christ are identified as the Word of God. Learn how Jesus endorsed the authority of Scripture and how to use God's Word as a two-edged sword yourself.

3. Through Repentance to Faith
What is faith? And how can you develop it? It starts with repentance: to change the way we think and to begin acting accordingly.

4. Faith and Works

Many Christians live in a kind of twilight - halfway between law and grace. They do not know which is which nor how to avail themselves of God's grace.

5. The Doctrine of Baptisms

A baptism is a transition - out of an old way of living into a totally new way of living. All of our being is involved. This study explains the baptism of John and the Christian (water) baptism. The baptism in the Holy Spirit is explained in 'Immersion in the Spirit'.

6. Immersion in the Spirit

Immersion can be accomplished in two ways: the swimming pool way and the Niagara Falls way. This book takes a closer look at the Niagara Falls experience, which relates to the baptism of the Holy Spirit.

7. Transmitting God's Power

Laying on of hands is one of the basic tenets of the Christian faith. By it, we may transmit God's blessing and authority and commission someone for service. Discover this Biblical doctrine!

8. At The End of Time

In this study, Derek Prince reveals the nature of eternity and outlines what lies ahead in the realm of end-time events.

9. Resurrection of the Body

The death and resurrection of Jesus produced a change in the universe. Derek explains here how the resurrection of Jesus impacted man's spirit, soul, and body.

10. Final Judgment

This book examines the four major, successive scenes of judgment in eternity. Exploring the distinctive aspects of these four judgments, Derek opens the Scriptures to bring forth treasures hidden there.

Christian Foundations Course

If you have enjoyed this study and would like to deepen your knowledge of God's Word and apply the teaching – why not enrol on Derek Prince's Christian Foundations Bible Course?

Building on the Foundations of God's Word

A detailed study of the six essential doctrines of Christianity found in Hebrews 6:1-2.

- Scripture-based curriculum
- Practical, personal application
- Systematic Scripture memorisation
- Opportunity for questions and personal feedback from course tutor
- Certificate upon completion
- Modular based syllabus
- Set your own pace
- Affordable
- Based on *Foundational Truths for Christian Living.*

For a prospectus, application form and pricing information, please visit www.dpmuk.org, call 01462 492100 or send an e-mail to enquiries@dpmuk.org

Foundational Truths
For Christian Living

Develop a strong, balanced, Spirit-filled life, by discovering the foundations of faith: salvation; baptism, the Holy Spirit, laying on hands, the believers' resurrection and eternal judgment.

Its reader-friendly format includes a comprehensive index of topics and a complete index of Scripture verses used in the book.

ISBN 978-1-908594-82-2
Paperback and eBook
£ 13.99

www.dpmuk.org/shop

More best-sellers by Derek Prince

- Blessing or Curse: You can Choose
- Bought with Blood
- Life-Changing Spiritual Power
- Marriage Covenant
- Prayers & Proclamations
- Self-Study Bible Course
- Shaping History Through Prayer and Fasting
- Spiritual Warfare for the End Times
- They Shall Expel Demons
- Who is the Holy Spirit?

For more titles: www.dpmuk.org/shop

Inspired by Derek's teaching?

Help make it available to others!

If you have been inspired and blessed by this Derek Prince resource you can help make it available to a spiritually hungry believer in other countries, such as China, the Middle East, India, Africa or Russia.

Even a small gift from you will ensure that that a pastor, Bible college student or a believer elsewhere in the world receives a free copy of a Derek Prince resource in their own language.

**Donate now: www.dpmuk.org/give
or visit www.derekprince.com**

Derek Prince Ministries

DPM–Asia/Pacific
38 Hawdon Street
Sydenham
Christchurch 8023
New Zealand
T: + 64 3 366 4443
E: admin@dpm.co.nz
W: www.dpm.co.nz

DPM–Australia
15 Park Road
Seven Hills
New South Wales 2147
Australia
T: +61 2 9838 7778
E: enquiries@au.derekprince.com
W: www.derekprince.com.au

DPM–Canada
P. O. Box 8354
Halifax
Nova Scotia B3K 5M1
Canada
T: + 1 902 443 9577
E: enquiries.dpm@eastlink.ca
W: www.derekprince.org

DPM–France
B.P. 31, Route d'Oupia
34210 Olonzac
France
T: + 33 468 913872
E: info@derekprince.fr
W: www.derekprince.fr

DPM–Germany
Söldenhofstr. 10
83308 Trostberg
Germany
T: + 49 8621 64146
E: ibl@ibl-dpm.net
W: www.ibl-dpm.net

DPM-Netherlands
Nijverheidsweg 12
7005 BJ, Doetinchem
Netherlands
T: +31 251-255044
E: info@derekprince.nl
W: www.derekprince.nl

Offices Worldwide

DPM–Norway
P. O. Box 129
Lodderfjord
N-5881 Bergen
Norway
T: +47 928 39855
E: xpress@dpskandinavia.com
W: www.derekprince.no

Derek Prince Publications Pte. Ltd.
P. O. Box 2046
Robinson Road Post Office
Singapore 904046
T: + 65 6392 1812
E: dpmchina@singnet.com.sg
W: www.dpmchina.org (English)
       www.ygmweb.org (Chinese)

DPM–South Africa
P. O. Box 33367
Glenstantia
0010 Pretoria
South Africa
T: +27 12 348 9537
E: enquiries@derekprince.co.za
W: www.derekprince.co.za

DPM–Switzerland
Alpenblick 8
CH-8934 Knonau
Switzerland
T: + 41 44 768 25 06
E: dpm-ch@ibl-dpm.net
W: www.ibl-dpm.net

DPM–UK
PO Box 393
Hitchin SG5 9EU
United Kingdom
T: + 44 1462 492100
E: enquiries@dpmuk.org
W: www.dpmuk.org

DPM–USA
P. O. Box 19501
Charlotte NC 28219
USA
T: + 1 704 357 3556
E: ContactUs@derekprince.org
W: www.derekprince.org